Parrot Parrot

Edited by Linda Meyer and Fiona Tang

Paperback ISBN: 978-1-943241-04-0
EPUB ISBN: 978-1-943241-09-5
Mobipocket ISBN: 978-1-943241-24-8
ePDF ISBN: 978-1-943241-28-6

Library of Congress Control Number: 2015943300

Phonic Monic Books
www.phonicmonic.com

C&C Joint Printing Co. (Guangdong) Ltd.
Chunhu Industrial Eatate, Pinghu
Long Gang, Shenzhen, PRC 518111
www.candcprinting.com

First Edition – April 2016

Image Credits:
Cover pg. Mayskyphoto/Shutterstock, Editor pg. panbazil/Shutterstock, Dedication pg. Natthawat Wongrat/Shutterstock, keng88/Shutterstock; 1, yayalineage/Shutterstock; 2, Rosa Jay/Shutterstock; 3, Rosa Jay/Shutterstock; 4, Rosa Jay/Shutterstock; 5, Bryoni Castelijn/Shutterstock; 6, Lindsey Eltinge/Shutterstock; 7, MustafaNC/Shutterstock; 8, Lindsey Eltinge/Shutterstock; 9 , Super Prin/Shutterstock; 10, Natali Glado/Shutterstock; 11, Tracy Starr/Shutterstock; 12, jurra8/Shutterstock; 13, JMiks/Shutterstock; 14, aaltair/Shutterstock; 15, Wiratchai wansamngam/Shutterstock; 16, Butterfly Hunter/Shutterstock; 17, Tracy Starr/Shutterstock; 18, Tracy Starr/Shutterstock; 19, duangnapa_b/Shutterstock; 20, duangnapa_b/Shutterstock; 21, Catmando/Shutterstock; 22, Ermolaev Alexander/Shutterstock; 23, Giancarlo Liguori/Shutterstock; 24, Miroslav Halama/Shutterstock; 25, Rosa Jay/Shutterstock; 26, YK/Shutterstock; 27, keng88/Shutterstock; 28, Panu Ruangjan/Shutterstock; 29, Catmando/Shutterstock; 31, TravnikovStudio/Shutterstock; 32, f9photos/Shutterstock; 33.

This book is dedicated to my friend Fiona Tang.
Thanks for all your support!

Parrot, parrot,

Eggs in a batch.

Parrot, parrot,

You can hatch.

Parrot, parrot,

On the ground.

Parrot, parrot,

Walk around.

Parrot, parrot,

Nice fine weather.

Parrot, parrot,

Grow your feathers.

Parrot, parrot,

All around.

Parrot, parrot,

Feathers fall down.

Parrot, parrot,

Just relax.

Parrot, parrot,

Feathers grow back.

Parrot, parrot,

Look at you now!

You're a big parrot!

Wow!

Parrot, parrot,

Colorful.

Parrot, parrot,

Beautiful.

Parrot, parrot,

Red and blue.

Parrot, parrot,

Green and yellow, too.

Parrot, parrot,

Nice curved beak.

Parrot, parrot,

Sharp clawed feet.

Parrot, parrot,

Do your thing.

Parrot, parrot,

Flap your wings.

Parrot, parrot,

Fly so high.

Parrot, parrot,

In the sky.

Parrot, parrot,

You can talk.

Parrot, parrot,

Squawk, squawk, squawk!

Parrot, parrot,

Hungry indeed.

Parrot, parrot,

Eat fruits and seeds.

Parrot, parrot,

Lay eggs in a batch.

One day, one day,

Eggs will hatch.

About the Author

Cammie Ho lives with her husband and two children in California, where she studied and obtained her Elementary School Teaching Credential and her Master's Degree in Teaching English as a Second Language.

Cammie loves reading books to her children, and is inspired by her favorite children's book authors, Dr. Seuss and Bill Martin Jr. She is developing an early learning program using music and chants to teach young children, believing that children learn well through a variety of fun channels. She writes lyrics and produces songs that teach reading and spelling in a program called, Phonic Monic.

www.phonicmonic.com